COMPUTER PIONEERS

Alan Turing

Master of Cracking Codes

Ryan Nagelhout

PowerKiDS press.

New York

Published in 2017 by The Rosen Publishing Group, Inc.
29 East 21st Street, New York, NY 10010

First Edition

Editor: Caitlin McAneney
Book Design: Mickey Harmon

Photo Credits: Cover, pp. 1, 3–16, 18–32 (background) yxowert/Shutterstock.com; cover, p. 9 (Alan Turning) Heritage Images/Contributor/Hulton Archive/Getty Images; p. 5 https://en.wikipedia.org/wiki/Alan_Turing#/media/File:Alan_Turing_Memorial_Closer.jpg; p. 7 Jeremy Walker/Britain on View/Getty Images; p. 8 https://en.wikipedia.org/wiki/Albert_Einstein#/media/File:Einstein_1921_by_F_Schmutzer_-_restoration.jpg; p. 11 courtesy of The Turing Digital Archive; p. 13 Rolf Richardson/Robert Harding World Imagery/Getty Images; p. 15 JEWEL SAMAD/Staff/AFP/Getty Images; p. 16 http://www.bletchleyparkresearch.co.uk/wp-content/uploads/2015/02/Joan-Clarke-Murray-1936.png).jpg; p. 17 https://en.wikipedia.org/wiki/Bombe#/media/File:Bletchley_Park_Bombe4.jpg; pp. 19, 21 Science & Society Picture Library/Contributor/SSPL/Getty Images; p. 23 https://en.wikipedia.org/wiki/Royal_Society#/media/File:Royal_Society_entrance.jpg; p. 25 (Alan Turing) https://commons.wikimedia.org/wiki/Category:Alan_Turing#/media/File:Alan_Turing_az_1930-as_%C3%A9vekben.jpg; p. 25 (Oscar Wilde inset) Everett Historical/Shutterstock.com; p. 27 https://en.wikipedia.org/wiki/Alan_Turing#/media/File:Turing_Plaque.jpg; p. 29 https://en.wikipedia.org/wiki/Alan_Turing#/media/File:Alan_Turing_Building_1.jpg.

Library of Congress Cataloging-in-Publication Data

Nagelhout, Ryan, author.
 Alan Turing : master of cracking codes/ Ryan Nagelhout.
    pages cm. — (Computer pioneers)
 Includes bibliographical references and index.
 ISBN 978-1-5081-4829-6 (pbk.)
 ISBN 978-1-5081-4768-8 (6 pack)
 ISBN 978-1-5081-4811-1 (library binding)
 1. Turing, Alan Mathison, 1912-1954—Juvenile literature. 2. Mathematicians—Great Britain—Biography—Juvenile literature. 3. Computer scientists—Great Britain—Biography—Juvenile literature. I. Title.
 QA29.T8N34 2016
 510.92—dc23
 [B]
                                          2015026658

Contents

The Secret Pioneer 4

Quiet and Alone 6

Friendship and Death 8

The Decision Problem 10

Captain Ridley's Shooting Party 12

Enigma and Bombe 14

America and the War's End 18

The ACE 20

The Test 22

Trial and Death 24

Knew Too Much? 26

Discovering the Genius....................... 28

Glossary 31

Index 32

Websites 32

The Secret Pioneer

The word "pioneer" often brings to mind explorers traveling to unknown places. Alan Turing was a different kind of pioneer. As a mathematician, his pioneering work was mostly done with numbers and often in secret. Turing is the father of modern computing. He did groundbreaking work in the field of **artificial intelligence**. He also saved millions of lives thanks to his code breaking during World War II.

With Turing's help, computers became a weapon just as powerful as the bombs, planes, and guns that fought the battles of World War II. His ideas and work laid the foundation for computers and technology he could only dream of during his lifetime. His efforts were kept secret for decades, but people have finally learned about his huge impact on the world.

Modern computers and artificial intelligence wouldn't exist without the work of Alan Turing. This statue of Turing honors his groundbreaking work.

Quiet and Alone

Alan Mathison Turing was born on June 23, 1912, in Maida Vale, London. Turing's parents—Julius and Ethel—lived in India, but Alan was born while they were visiting London. His father worked as an official for the British government in India, which Britain controlled at the time.

Turing and his older brother, John, spent most of their early life away from their parents. Rather than taking Alan back to India with them, his parents sent him to live with a retired army couple in Britain. When Turing was 13, he was sent to Sherborne School, a boarding school in Dorset. Turing wasn't popular at school. He was a bit clumsy and didn't do very well in his classes.

School Woes

Turing wasn't a good student at Sherborne School. He wasn't interested in English and was at the bottom of his class in most subjects. Even in math and science, his teacher complained, "His work is dirty." The headmaster of Sherborne School had trouble with Turing as well. He wrote that Turing was "the sort of boy who is bound to be a problem for any school or community."

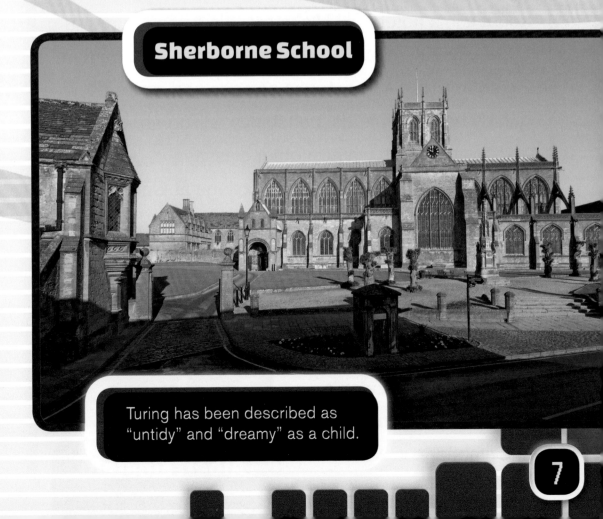

Sherborne School

Turing has been described as "untidy" and "dreamy" as a child.

Friendship and Death

Things changed for Turing when he turned 16. A year earlier, his grandfather gave him a copy of Albert Einstein's book, which described a complex theory. He read it and very quickly understood the theory, writing about it in a notebook. His interest in science grew in 1928 when he met Christopher Morcom, a student at Sherborne also interested in science and math. They quickly became friends, constantly talking about math and science even while in other classes.

The two planned to go to college at Cambridge together, but Morcom died suddenly on February 13, 1930. Turing was crushed, but he took the loss as a way to inspire himself to learn more. He won a scholarship to King's College at Cambridge in 1931.

Albert Einstein

Turing's friendship with Morcom helped him fall in love with science and apply himself more at school.

The Decision Problem

Turing did well at King's College and even became a **fellow** at age 22 in 1935. One day, while out on a run, Turing laid down in a meadow and came up with the idea for a machine to solve the "decision problem." The decision problem asked whether **logic** and reasoning could be reduced to a simple math problem.

Turing imagined a machine that could be built to break problems down into a set of numbers using various instructions. The machine would have a long strip of tape divided into small squares called cells. A scanner would move back and forth over the cells, changing numbers based on what was in the cell and what state the machine was operating in. The **theoretical** device, soon called the Turing machine, could perform all kinds of mathematical problems.

Alan Turing

At age 23, Turing realized a machine couldn't solve the decision problem. Though the decision problem was impossible for a machine to solve, Turing decided it was possible to make a "universal" Turing machine that could run different programs.

Make-Believe Machine?

Turing machines are theoretical, meaning they don't actually exist. A Turing machine is an imaginary model of a computer that can read and write symbols on a strip of tape and has a limitless amount of information storage. A set of directions tells the machine how to function. Turing showed that—as long as the machine knows its commands and there's a long enough piece of tape—his theoretical machine could calculate anything.

Captain Ridley's Shooting Party

In 1938, Turing earned a Ph.D. in mathematics from Princeton University in New Jersey. He then returned to Cambridge. World War II began on September 1, 1939, when **Nazi** Germany invaded Poland. Great Britain joined the war, and three days later, Turing left Cambridge for Bletchley Park, a sprawling compound northwest of London. Turing joined "Captain Ridley's Shooting Party," which was a secret name for a massive **intelligence** effort organized by Britain's government and military.

The "party" was a group of code breakers who were brought together with one purpose: to crack the codes and **ciphers** used by the Nazi military to communicate in secret. Because the mission at Bletchley Park was kept secret, many people wondered why so many able-bodied men were there instead of serving in the military.

Nazi Codes

Codes and ciphers are used during wartime to send messages about troop movement and other important plans that should be kept from the enemy. **Encrypted** codes could be sent over public communications safely without an enemy understanding them. Bletchley Park set out to crack numerous Nazi codes, including those produced on a device called the Enigma machine. The German navy's Enigma codes, particularly those used by its submarines, or U-boats, were thought to be unbreakable.

Captain Ridley's Shooting Party was established by Britain's intelligence service (M16), the British military, and the Government Code and Cypher School (GC&CS).

Enigma and Bombe

Many different codes were tackled at Bletchley Park, but Enigma codes were Turing's obsession. German U-boats were **blockading** the British Islands, sinking about 60 of the **Allies**' ships each month as they tried to get supplies to Britain. The British people were on the brink of starving unless there was some way to know where the U-boats were heading.

Working in Hut 8 at Bletchley Park, Turing noticed some parts of code were often repeated, such as the phrase "weather for the night." Figuring this piece out eliminated billions of possible machine settings. Turing thought he could make a machine that could go through the code looking for these bits of code and help the code breakers work faster. This machine let code breakers crack Enigma messages before its code changed for the day.

How Enigma Worked

The Enigma machine looked like a typewriter. Words typed on its keyboard had their letters scrambled by little wheels inside the machine. The scrambled code could be sent out over the radio in the form of long and short signals using a system called Morse code. Anyone with an Enigma machine set to the same wheel settings could type it in and translate the message back to plain language. Enigma codes used by Nazi U-boats changed every day, so Turing had to crack a different code every 24 hours.

The Enigma machine was so complex its keys were said to make around 150 quintillion different combinations. That's 150,000,000,000,000,000,000 different ways to code messages!

Turing created a machine with dozens of spinning drums that imitated the wheels in the Enigma machine. The machine was loud and huge. Turing called it a Bombe, in honor of a Polish code-breaking machine called "bomba" because it made a loud ticking sound. By 1941, Bletchley Park had 18 Bombes cracking all kinds of Nazi Enigma codes.

On some days, the code could be broken in about an hour. This helped the Allies learn where Nazi troops and U-boats were, where they were heading, and how to avoid or counterattack their actions. As Nazi missions began to fail, their top officials suspected **espionage** inside the German army. No one could believe their code had been broken.

Turing was briefly engaged to Joan Clarke, a mathematician who worked at Bletchley Park. However, the two never married.

copy of the Bombe

America and the War's End

Turing helped Bletchley Park adapt to changes German scientists made to the Enigma machine as the war continued. Once the Enigma codes were consistently broken, Turing moved to the United States to help with American code-breaking efforts. He taught the Americans how to make their own Bombes and explained what he knew about the Enigma machine. In 1943, he also helped Bell Laboratories work on a speech encryption program.

The mathematicians and code breakers at Bletchley Park kept working on other codes as the war continued. Later, Turing returned to Buckinghamshire, England, to help with Colossus, another code-breaking machine. World War II ended on September 2, 1945. One British historian says the work at Bletchley Park shortened the war by two to four years, and, without it, the Allies might not have won.

Turing was brilliant, and his machines were revolutionary. But he was also known at Bletchley Park for being a bit odd. He wore a gas mask when he rode his bike to help with his allergies.

The ACE

Turing worked at Britain's National Physical Laboratory (NPL) after World War II ended. Later in 1945, he proposed building a Universal Machine, which was a similar but much more advanced model of the Turing machines he imagined at Cambridge. The detailed design even included diagrams for electrical circuits. The design for the Automatic Computing Engine (ACE) was approved in 1946, but Turing struggled with limited resources at NPL.

Turing left for a position directing a different computer model at Manchester University in 1948. A working version of his design was made at NPL in 1950. Called the Pilot ACE, it was the first stored-program computer in Britain. By then, Turing was working on much more complex ideas about artificial intelligence.

A stored-program computer keeps software, or computer programs, in its electronic memory. The Pilot ACE is still on display at the Science Museum in London, England.

World-Class Runner

Turing enjoyed long-distance running throughout his life. He joined running clubs and even won a few races. In 1948, he ran a marathon (26.2 miles, 42.2 km) in 2 hours, 46 minutes, 3 seconds. That was just 11 minutes slower than the Olympic-winning marathon time later that year. He would run between the two places he worked, often beating coworkers who took public transportation. Turing said running helped him unwind from his stressful job.

The Test

In 1950, Turing published a paper entitled "Computing Machinery and Intelligence" in the philosophy journal *Mind*. Turing wanted to determine if machines could really think. He even proposed a way to test a machine's ability to think called the "imitation game."

A person asks questions in writing to what's either a machine or human. The questions will reveal if the computer has or lacks human thought. For the modern Turing Test, if a computer is mistaken for a human being more than 30 percent of the time in 5 minutes, the machine passes and is said to be "thinking." In 2014—more than 60 years after he proposed it—a machine passed the Turing Test for the first time.

In 1951, Turing was elected a Fellow of the Royal Society for his work in science.

Morphogenesis

Turing wasn't just a mathematician—he also invented a completely new field of biology. Called morphogenesis, it's the mathematical study of how things grow. In 1951, Turing wrote a paper about the topic called "The Chemical Basis of Morphogenesis." The paper presented a model for how cells change as they grow. It's been cited thousands of times by other researchers. Sixty years later, scientists studying morphogenesis said they found evidence that Turing's original ideas were right!

Trial and Death

In 1952, Turing called the police when someone broke into his house. In speaking to the British police, he admitted to having a relationship with a man. Homosexuality was a crime in Britain at this time, so rather than find who broke into his home, the police arrested Turing. At a trial, Turing was **convicted** of "gross indecency."

The punishment was either two years in prison or a "treatment program" where Turing was injected with chemicals. Turing chose the terrible treatments as part of his sentence. He was also labeled as dangerous and could no longer work in the labs where he was developing computer technology. Two years after being labeled a criminal, Turing died. He was 41.

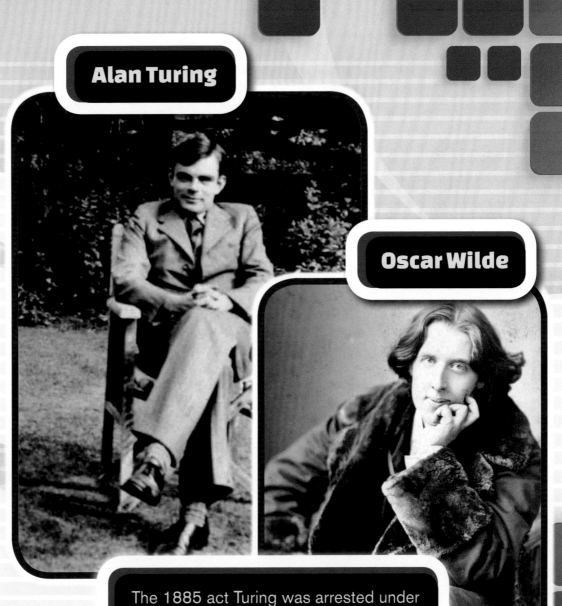

Alan Turing

Oscar Wilde

The 1885 act Turing was arrested under was the same one under which British author Oscar Wilde was arrested and sent to prison in 1895.

Knew Too Much?

The investigation into Turing's death ruled that he poisoned himself with a chemical called cyanide. An apple with a few bites missing was found near Turing's body, so it was assumed he poisoned the apple himself. However, others believe his death may have been an accident. Turing was performing experiments with many chemicals at home, and his mother believed he accidentally ate or breathed in something that killed him.

Some people even wonder if Turing was secretly killed by someone else. Turing was part of many secret projects before and after the war. After his arrest, he was traveling quite a bit, and some **biographers** suggest people were nervous about his actions. No one ever tested the apple found by Turing's body for cyanide, so no one knows for sure how he died.

ALAN TURING
1912 - 1954

Founder of computer science and cryptographer, whose work was key to breaking the wartime Enigma codes, lived and died here.

Turing was thought to be sloppy, so some think he may have accidentally poisoned himself.

Discovering the Genius

Today, more than 150,000 people visit Bletchley Park each year. Turing's work during the war was kept secret until the 1970s, meaning most people knew nothing of his heroic code-breaking efforts while he was alive.

On December 24, 2013, Alan Turing was officially given a royal pardon by the British monarchy for his arrest and conviction. An online petition started in 2011 got more than 34,000 signatures and gained support from famous scientists like Dr. Stephen Hawking. Turing was also given a public apology in 2009 from then-British prime minister Gordon Brown. In 2014, his life was made into a movie called *The Imitation Game*. Years after being labeled a criminal, Turing is rightfully seen as the hero and genius who helped win a war and change the world forever.

Alan Turing Building
University of Manchester
Manchester, England

Turing's scientific ideas and technological breakthroughs are still cited today, and the Turing Test is the benchmark still used in the development of artificial intelligence.

Timeline

1912
Turing is born in London on June 23.

1926
Turing attends Sherborne School until 1931.

1928
Turing meets Christopher Morcom.

1930
Christopher Morcom dies suddenly.

1931
Turing attends King's College, Cambridge University.

1935
Turing is elected a King's College fellow.

1936
Turing imagines the Turing machine.

1936
Turing moves to America and attends Princeton University.

1938
Turing earns his Ph.D. in mathematics at Princeton University.

1939
World War II begins on Sept. 1. Turing begins work at Bletchley Park.

1941
Eighteen Bombes are running at Bletchley Park.

1943
Turing travels to America to help code breakers there.

1945
World War II ends on Sept. 2. Turing proposes plans for ACE.

1950
Pilot ACE computer is finished. Turing proposes Turing Test.

1951
Turing is elected a Fellow of the Royal Society.

1952
Turing is arrested and tried for "indecency."

1954
Turing dies on June 7.

Glossary

Allies: The group of nations, including England and the United States, in World War II that opposed the Axis nations, including Germany and Japan.

artificial intelligence: An area of computer science that deals with giving machines the ability to "think."

biographer: Someone who records the story of a person's life.

blockade: Cutting off an area by means of ships to stop the coming and going of people and supplies.

cipher: A secret way of writing; a code. Also spelled "cypher."

convict: To find or prove guilty of a crime.

encrypted: Converted into a code.

espionage: The practice of spying.

fellow: A person granted funds for advanced study.

intelligence: The gathering of secret information about enemies.

logic: A proper or reasonable way of thinking about or understanding something.

Nazi: Pertaining to the National Socialist German Workers' Party, which led Germany from 1933 until 1945, when World War II ended.

theoretical: Based on thought and calculation rather than physical proof.

Index

A
ACE, 20, 30
artificial intelligence, 4, 5, 20, 29

B
Bell Laboratories, 18
Bletchley Park, 12, 13, 14, 16, 18, 19, 28, 30
Bombe, 16, 17, 18, 30

C
Cambridge, 8, 12, 20, 30
code breakers, 12, 14, 30
Colossus, 18
"Computing Machinery and Intelligence," 22

D
death, 24, 26, 30
decision problem, 10, 11

E
Enigma codes, 13, 14, 16, 18
Enigma machine, 13, 15, 16, 18

I
imitation game, 22
Imitation Game, The, 28

K
King's College, 8, 10, 30

M
Manchester University, 20, 29
Morcom, Christopher, 8, 9, 30
morphogenesis, 23

N
NPL, 20

P
pardon, 28
Pilot ACE, 20, 21, 30
Princeton University, 12, 30

S
Sherborne School, 6, 7, 8, 30

T
trial, 24
Turing machine, 10, 11, 20, 30
Turing Test, 22, 29, 30

U
United States, 18
Universal Machine, 20

W
World War II, 4, 12, 18, 30

Websites

Due to the changing nature of Internet links, PowerKids Press has developed an online list of websites related to the subject of this book. This site is updated regularly. Please use this link to access the list: www.powerkidslinks.com/compio/alan